IDENTIFICATION

WITH CHRIST

DELIVERANCE:
MAN'S WAY IS TO SUPRESS SIN.
GOD'S WAY IS TO REMOVE SIN.

Copyright © 2019 by Curry R. Blake

All Rights Reserved

Published by

CHRISTIAN REALITY BOOKS
P.O. Box 742947
Dallas TX 75374
1-888-293-6591

Unless otherwise noted, all Scripture quotations are taken from the King James Bible.

This book or parts thereof may not be reproduced in any form without express written permission of Curry Blake.

Printed in the United States of America.

"Christ's Total Gospel for the Total Deliverance of the Total Man."

By
Wilford H. Reidt

Foreword

The book you are about to read was originally designed to be a course in John Lake's "School of The Prophets" Bible School in 1934. Most people remember John Lake because of his phenomenal healing ministry, but Lake himself often referred to being a new creation as the reason for his successful results in healing and miracles. Wilford Reidt knew John Lake from 1931 until Lake's death in 1935. When Lake began preparations for a short-term bible school, he enlisted the help of Wilford to prepare the courses. Together, John Lake and Wilford Reidt constructed the courses from Lake's sermons and notes. The outlines they authored have never before been published.

Now for the first time, we are releasing the material meant for training ministers. After Lake's death, Wilford wrote this book from the notes and conversations he had with John Lake concerning the Christian's Identification With Christ.
In 1941, Wilford married Lake's daughter, Gertrude. Together, they gathered all the material they could find concerning John Lake. Shortly before they passed away, Wilford sent me all the material they had and gave me permission to publish the material as I saw fit.

I have now begun publishing the material in its unedited form. As you read "Identification With Christ" by Wilford Reidt, you will see the level of John Lake's revelation of who we are in Christ and you will see how that understanding was far in advance of where the majority of Christians were in 1934 (and even where Christians are today in their understanding). Furthermore, you will see how God has been trying to get this understanding into the Body of Christ for decades.

    As you read this book, prayerfully expect The Spirit of God to open the eyes of your understanding and give you the Spirit of wisdom and revelation in the knowledge of God. He desires for you to walk in the fullness of this revelation even more than you do.

He wanted it so much, He gave His Son's life to purchase it, so you can have it!

Blessings,
Curry R. Blake

IDENTIFICATION WITH CHRIST

Wilford Reidt

"I have just been born into the family of God. What does God really think of me? How does He really feel?"

Do you suppose God looked upon you and exclaimed to the angels, "What a dirty, filthy, imperfect kid!"? Do you think the angels would have rejoiced?

"Surely, God did see me like that after the blood of Jesus cleansed me from all my sins."

You are right. God looked upon you with great joy and sang over you (Zephaniah 3:17). He looked upon you and saw you as a beautiful baby in Jesus. He saw you as lovely and perfect. There was rejoicing in heaven (Luke 15:7).

You are now a new-born babe in the family of God. You are born into His family (John 3:3). He wants you to be absolutely certain of this. To be sure, in the ultimate sense, He also adopted you (Romans 8:15). Now you are doubly His child.

You are now experiencing the greatest thing in the whole creation, the love of God. You are now launching out on an exciting adventure with Him. You are going to grow up into Him (Jesus) in all things (Ephesians 4:15).

To help you to be the best God desires, He has provided some ministries to help you in your growth. "And he gave some, apostles; and some, prophets; and some, evangelists; and some pastors and teachers; for the perfecting of the saints, for the work of the ministry, for the edifying (building up) of the body of Christ" (Eph. 4:11-13).

Be sure you follow the Lord in water baptism. "This is immersion because you want to be buried with Him in baptism. "Therefore, we are buried with him by baptism into death…" (Romans 6:4). The significance of this we will discuss later.

God has another great gift for you. He desires to baptize you in the Holy Spirit according to the pattern set forth in Acts 2:4 and Acts 10:44-46. This is the Comforter spoken of by Jesus. "But the Comforter, which is the Holy Ghost (Holy Spirit) whom the Father will send in my name, he will teach you <u>all things</u>…" (John 14:26). This can come through any of the ministries spoken of above or by direct teaching while you study the Word. Usually it is a combination of all of these. The study of the Holy Spirit is a subject in itself and is not a part of the subject being dealt with.

Probably one of the hardest things you will have to get settled down into the very fiber of your being is that all your past sins are forgiven and forgotten. "And their sins and iniquities will I remember no more" (Hebrews 10:17). You are now justified by His blood (Romans 5:9). It is as someone has said, "Just as if you had never sinned." It is good to become thoroughly acquainted with this, as it is one of the devil's tricks to bring up the past. He uses it to try to discourage you. The scriptures we have just quoted are a part of the "sword of the Spirit." (Eph. 6:17). Quote them to the devil. He can't stand the Word. In this response to Satan you are using the Word to resist him, and he will have to flee from you (James 4:7). In our personal growth we forget those things that are behind and press to the mark of the high calling of God (Philippians 3:13). You may use your past in testimony to show what God has done for you. It will be a help to others and will encourage them to seek deliverance.

    The love of God is so great it staggers the intellect. While you were a sinner and unlovely in God's sight, He sent His Son to be your Savior (Romans 5:8). Now that you are a child of God He loves you with His Son Jesus. "And hast loved them, as thou hast loved me" (John 17:23). You ask in amazement, "How can we grasp the scope of God's love?" "And to know the love of Christ, which passeth knowledge, that ye might be filled with all the fullness of God" (Ephesians 3:19). How can you know that love? You will know it by experience as you grow up in Him.

    "Let us go back a bit. You said that God saw me as perfect. Come on now! How can that be?" The word "perfect" is from a Greek word that means <u>complete</u>. You were born a complete baby in Christ. It is the perfection of babyhood.

    At this point we will offer an illustration. The farmer goes out to his orchard and takes the fading blossom of an apple tree and peels it back. A tiny apple is exposed and he declares it is perfect. A few weeks later he again looks at the same apple. It has grown, and it is still perfect in His sight. It was said of Jesus, "and being made perfect…" (Hebrews 5:8). He was perfect and being made perfect. Take His words for the final clincher, "But everyone that is perfect shall be as his master" (Luke 6:40). You are perfect and being made perfect. As a newborn babe you are clean because of the cleansing power of Jesus' blood (Revelation 1:5). Now you can understand why the word "imperfect" is not used in the Bible.

We are feeding you with the milk of the Word so that you may grow. "As newborn babes, desire the sincere milk of the word that ye may grow thereby" (1 Peter 2:2). Don't be afraid to ask questions. They are one of the greatest tools of learning. We will be careful not to depart from "the simplicity that is in Christ" (2 Corinthians 11:3). Terms used will be carefully defined so you will know exactly what is being said.

"What happened to me when I was born into the Kingdom of God? What is it that made me a new creation? I read in 2 Corinthians 5:17, "Therefore if any man be in Christ, he is a new creature: old things are passed away; behold, all things are become new." There is a pattern. Jesus is the beginning of this new race, this new creation. He is the head of the body (Colossians 1:18). "And have put on the new man, which is renewed in knowledge after the image of him (Jesus) that created him (you)" (Colossians 3:10). You see, Jesus was born of the Virgin Mary. He was born with a pure human nature. This pure human nature was united with the Divine Nature in Jesus. This made Him the God-man. When you were born again, God cleansed your nature by the blood of Jesus. He then united your pure nature with the divine nature. You are now a partaker of the divine nature. (2 Peter 1:4). That is the new creation. It is patterned after Jesus. "Old things are passed away." The words "are passed" refer to an act that took place and result is still in effect. In you there is a union of the human and the divine. That is why it says in 1 Corinthians 6:17, "But he that is joined to the Lord is one spirit."

As you grow and become stronger you will come to the place where you will take your first step of faith. Let us make a comparison. Here is a young couple. Their child takes its first step, then stumbles and falls. They are delighted and love the little fellow. They do not punish him for stumbling and falling. Why not? They know that he will eventually learn to walk. It is the same with our Heavenly Father. He is delighted at your first step. One of our problems is the people who expect the newborn believer to walk as an adult believer. They are ever ready with a criticism, with a condemning word. They look on your failure to take the second step with a critical eye. They didn't treat their children that way when they were growing up. We say this to put you on your guard. When you hear them, just let it go in one ear and out the other. They need to learn compassion and patience.

One thing we want you to learn early is that you don't have to sin. "My little children, these things write I unto you, that ye sin not" (1 John 2:1). It is one of the devil's tricks to get a younger believer to sin and then to pile condemnation on him. He makes you feel like you have done so terribly that God is through with you, that God is really mad at you, that you have lost your salvation. He will keep up a steady flow of accusations. He even gets some to believe they are now lost. You ask in all sincerity, "What do I do? Have I lost my salvation?"

You are a growing believer. God is delighted in you. You have taken a step of faith. Then if the devil tricks you and you sin ignorantly or unawares, what should you do?

Repent.

God forgives and forgets (Hebrews 10; 17). Learn a lesson from it and watch that the devil does not do the same thing again.

Get up and go on with God. God understands. He is still with you. If you let Him, He will always lift you up just as any good father does. "If any man sin, we have an advocate with the Father, Jesus Christ the righteous: and he is the propitiation for our sins…" (1John 2:1-2). Jesus is your advocate (intercessor). He prays for you and God forgives.

The blood of Jesus cleanses away the stain caused by sin. "…And the blood of Jesus Christ his Son cleanseth us from all sin" (1 John 1:7). Purity of heart is restored. God is delighted in you. He sees you as perfect. You still have salvation.

Sometimes a person gets discouraged or depressed because of circumstances and is tempted. He gives in under pressure. It is willful: he knows better.

Two paths are open to him:

He may continue in the sin. This leads to a habit that in turn leads to fruitlessness. And this in turn leads to being cut out of the vine (John 15:2).

1. He may repent. God will forgive and restore him.

2. He may do as the prodigal son (Luke 15:11-32) and take off for a long time.

But remember the father didn't follow the prodigal son to rob him of his stuff or to put him in the pig pen. That all came as a result of his own choice.

But when the son had enough of the result of his sin, he returned to the father and was accepted back into the family with joy. It is Jeremiah 2:19 in action, "Thine own wickedness shall correct thee, and thy backslidings shall reprove thee." As you grow you will catch onto the tricks of the devil. Your senses will be exercised to discern both good and evil (Hebrews 5:14). You are learning to choose the good and refuse the evil. You will not be ignorant of his devices (2 Corinthians 2:11).

You are a growing child of God. He is delighted in your progress. You will notice that the Holy Spirit is revealing things in your life that need to be corrected as you go along. As you study Jesus and see Him in all His purity and beauty, there will be changes taking place in you. Some already have.

"But we all, with open face beholding as in a glass the glory of the Lord, are changed into the same image from glory to glory, even as by the Spirit of the Lord" (2 Corinthians 3:18). The word "changed" as used here is a metamorphosis. It is the same Greek word as "changed". It is a metamorphosis. As you see Jesus let the Holy Spirit lead you into all the truth (Jesus). "Howbeit when he, the Spirit of Truth, is come, he will guide you into all truth…" (John 16:13). As an example, I knew of a man who had a violent temper. After he was saved he still lost control. He tried and tried to control it, but it was of no use. He went down before God and presented his case to the Lord. He saw how Jesus was, and it was the desire of his heart to be like Him. In about a thirty-minute prayer the Holy Spirit performed a metamorphosis on his inner man, and never again did he lose his temper.

You see, he was changed from one state of glory (he had salvation) to a more glorious state in which he had salvation plus victory over his temper. Tests will show up the weaknesses in life, but tests and trials cannot change your inner being. It takes the Holy Spirit to do that. Testing a piece of metal will only show its strengths and weaknesses. The test does not make a change in the metal.

God delights to see you becoming like His Son. He loves you and is backing you, 100 percent.

I want you to know that you are giving your Heavenly Father a lot of pleasure.

There is another principle that should be taught early in the life of the believer. It is the principle of identification. Christ identified with us, so we can be identified with Him. He was made sin that we might be made the Righteousness of God" (2 Corinthians 5:21). He was made a curse for us that we could be redeemed from the curse of the law (Galatians 3:13). God's justice demanded a penalty for sin. "The soul that sinneth, it shall die" (Ezekiel 18:20). The penalty of sin is death, eternal separation from God. Jesus became sin and bore the penalty for us. He tasted death for every man (Hebrews 2:19). How did He do this? When He became sin, it separated Him from His Father. The agony of it was so great He cried, "…My God, my God, why hast thou forsaken me!' (Matthew 27:46). You see, Jesus not only tasted physical death but also spiritual separation (death) from the Father. He was resurrected out of this separation (death).

Now we can be resurrected out of our spiritual separation (death) from the Father. "Even when we were dead in sins, (God) hath <u>raised</u> <u>us</u> <u>up</u> <u>together</u> (Ephesians 2:5-6). Another presentation from John might help to clarify the idea. "And whosoever liveth and believeth in me shall never die" (John 11:26).

1. Whoever liveth:

We live because we are <u>raised</u> <u>up</u> <u>with</u> <u>Him</u>. "…Ye are risen with Him (Jesus) through the faith of the operation of God, who hath raised him from the dead" (Colossians 2:12). This is our resurrection from being spiritually dead to being spiritually alive, that is to have eternal life now. This happened at your new birth.

2. Shall never die:

We shall never be eternally separated from the Father. Jesus was also raised physically from the dead. We shall also be like Him in physical resurrection. "Behold my hands and my feet, that it is I myself: handle me and see; for a spirit hath not flesh and bones, as ye see me have" (Luke 24:39). "Who shall change our vile body that it may be fashioned like unto his glorious body…" (Philippians 3:21). "Vile" means depressed or humiliated in this setting. Now you can understand how Jesus identified with us that we might be identified with Him in life.

It seems necessary that we define a few terms and picture what happened to Adam and what Jesus, the second Adam, did to deliver mankind.

Fall	**Cross**	**"In the Flesh"**
Adam in the garden. A pure and holy man.	Human nature under the power of sin.	Delivered.
	Something added to man's nature that was not there before the fall.	Provision for deliverance from that something.

What is that something?
It is called "in the flesh" (human nature under the power of sin) (Romans 8:8).

- It is called the "principle of sin" by some, the spirit of rebellion.
- It is called the "old man" in Romans 6:6: Ephesians 4:22, and Colossians 3:9.

For simplicity's sake we will use mostly the term "old man" in our study.

What was the origin of the "old man?"
It was not Adam himself, as he was created in the image of God and was holy. Before Adam fell there was no "old man". Adam lived in a state of purity. When man fell, his nature came under the

power of sin. The spirit of rebellion was added to his nature. It is called the "old man". The object of our study now is to find out how to get rid of the "old man".

To get rid of something we should know what it is like. What is the "old man" like? What are his works?

The Works of the "Old Man"

Galatians 4:19-21		Ephesians 4:25, 29, 31:	
Adultery	Emulations	Lying	Evil speaking
Fornication	Wrath	Bitterness	Greediness
Uncleanness	Seditions	Colossians 3:5,8:	
Lasciviousness	Heresies	Clamor	Malice
Idolatry	Murders	Inordinate affection	Blasphemy
Witchcraft	Drunkenness	Evil concupiscence	Intemperance
Hatred	Revelings	Covetousness	Impatience
Variance		Anger	Unbelief
		Romans 14:23	
		Whatsoever is not of faith	

You cannot convert the "old man". You cannot clean him up. He is dirty and filthy. You must put him off. (Colossians 3:9) What is now being taught was legally accomplished for you in Christ. Now we wish to know how to make it vitally yours. Galatians 5:17-24 will be the basis for our study. It is here you get the contrast. It is found in verses 17 and 24: "For the flesh (the old man) lusteth against the Spirit, and the Spirit against the flesh: and these are contrary the one to the other: so that ye cannot do the things ye would" (Galatians 5:17).

The clash between the "old man" and the Spirit of God prevents you, or hinders you, from doing all you know God wants.

"And they that are Christ's have crucified the flesh (the old man) with the affections and lusts" (Galatians 5:24). With the flesh (the old man) crucified and dead, you can do <u>all</u> the will of God. This is done through identification. Newborn believers do not know the full impact of identification with Christ.

One man who had been saved only a month declared that he was puzzled and disturbed. Things were going on in his life that were hindering him spiritually. He was given a plain picture of identification. Now he knew where he stood in God. He understood what he had to do. He put the idea of identification into effect. Now he had the advantage over the devil. It helped to bring stability to his walk in God. How can one get rid of the "old man"? Remember that he is a part of the kingdom of darkness. He is the "spirit of rebellion" and can never be made subject to the will of God. Do not forget that you are a growing believer. God is delighted in you. He is now going to work something into your life that you will work out (Philippians 2:12, 13).

The process of getting rid of the "old man".
For the Jew and Gentile, Romans 6. Romans 7 is for those who are under the law. The Jew must die to the law.

Identification with Christ:

In His crucifixion:

I am crucified with Christ (Galatians 2:20).

Unto what am I crucified?
The world (Galatians 6:14).
What is crucified unto me?
The world (Galatians 6:14).

Who else was crucified with Christ?
The "old man" (Romans 6:6).

What part do I play in this?
You crucify the "flesh," the "old man" (Galatians 5:24). This is past tense showing you have done it.

What else do I do?

You put off the "old man" (Ephesians 4:22). "Put off" in the Greek has the same force as putting off your coat.

In His death: Before we can tell you how to <u>put off</u> the "old man" we must consider that crucifixion ends in death. That we died in Him is signified by being baptized into His death (Romans 6:4).

What did I die to?

Sin.

Jesus died unto sin <u>once</u> (Romans 6:10). When you identify with Him, you can <u>reckon</u> on that. "Likewise <u>reckon</u> ye also yourselves to be dead indeed unto sin…" (Romans 6;9,10).

The world (Galatians 6:14). This refers to the Kingdom of Darkness and all the old life in it. Crucified unto the world and the world unto you (Gal. 6:14). The world here will include the "old man" as he is a part of it. The "old man" was crucified with Christ and died with Him. Reckon him to be dead unto you. Reckon yourself to be dead unto him. Now you have <u>put</u> <u>him</u> <u>off</u> (Colossians 3:9). He died unto sin <u>once</u>. "Likewise reckon …yourselves to be dead…" "Likewise" means you need to die only once. Then operate from that standpoint. "He that is dead is freed from sin" (Romans 6:7).

In His burial:

Romans 6:4, "Buried with Him by baptism into death…"
(Colossians 2:12), "Buried with him by baptism…" Buried with Him in baptism signifies that the fact that you died with Him and now are buried with Him.

In His resurrection:

"Even when we were dead in sins, (God) hath quickened us together with Christ, (by grace are ye saved); and hath raised us up together (with Christ)…" (Ephesians 2:5-6).
"…Like that as Christ was raised up from the dead…even so we should walk in newness of life" (Romans 6:4).
"…Ye also are risen with him through the operation of God, who hath raised him (Jesus) from the dead" (Colossians 2:12).

There are several operations that are involved in your identification with Christ in His crucifixion, death, burial, and resurrection.

In the process God uses two methods:

Circumcision:

"In whom ye also are circumcised with the circumcision made without hands, in putting off the body of the sins of the flesh by the circumcision of Christ" (Colossians 2:11). "…Circumcision is that of the heart, in the spirit" (Romans 2:29).

The "body of the sins of the flesh" does not refer to your physical body, as you cannot put it off. The "old man" was crucified that the body of sins might be destroyed. (Romans 6:6).

Your part is to mortify (put to death) the deeds of the body (Romans 8:13). In doing so you put them off. God does the circumcising, does the inward work, and you work it out by cooperating, by mortification and putting off.

Metamorphosis:

But we all, with open face beholding as in a glass the glory of the Lord, are changed into the same image from glory to glory, even as by the Spirit of the Lord" (2 Cor. 3:18). The word, "change," is from a Greek word that means metamorphosis. Great things take place within you when you let the Spirit of God have His way. He demands total consecration.

Putting off the "old man" is not a lifetime process. Jesus' crucifixion did not take a lifetime. It was a short process. When you were saved, God cleansed you from all your sins. In identification, He removes the power of sin (the old man) out of you. He took you out of the world, and now He takes the world out of you. Satan has nothing in you. "If the Son therefore shall make you free, ye shall be free indeed" (John 8:36). "Behold the Lamb of God, which taketh away the sin of the world" (John 1:29).

Now that you have died to sin, operate from that standpoint. Satan is now fighting you from without. This is shown by Ephesians 6:16, "Above all taking the shield of faith, wherewith ye shall be able to quench all the fiery darts (missiles) of the wicked (devil)." He is shooting at you from without. He has no anchor within you. If you have a feeling of hate trying to come into you, reject it, as it is not coming out of your new nature. Respond by saying, "I am a new creation; my new nature is a love nature. I choose to love."

Satan now will try to get you to accept the evil thoughts he throws your way. Reject them. You cannot help a bird flying over your head, but you can keep it from making a nest in your hair. Reject the evil thoughts because they are not coming out of your new nature. You can now say with Jesus, "…For the prince of this world cometh, and hath nothing in me" (John 14:30).

Before we go further, as we consider crucifixion, the question will arise, "Does it not include suffering?" It involves putting the Lord first in your life. You may be tested on your weakest point to see if your consecration is genuine. This test will not come from Satan. It will come from God. He will not use Satan. He is big enough to take care of His own children without any help from His enemy. You can be sure the devil will try to stop you. But, you will push him aside and do what God asks of you. I will use an illustration of this. Remember that each person's test will be unique to himself. Abraham's test was unique to him. He was asked to offer up his son. He was allowed to proceed to the point he was willing; then God supplied another means of sacrifice.

Many years ago, I was acquainted with a lady who had laid all on God's altar and had put Him first in her life. One day the Spirit of God in prophecy told her to go to Spokane some 48 minutes away. He gave her the name of a funeral parlor and the time of the funeral. It was to be at 2:30. She and her husband went. It was a funeral of a little girl about her own daughter's age. Now came the thoughts, "Did you really mean it when you put Me first? Did you really mean it when you included your little girl?" She wept during that funeral as if it were her own daughter. Then she came to the point where she said to the Lord that she meant it. The test was over. A deep peace settled upon her. She had reached the point of commitment. Did she lose her daughter? No. Her daughter is still living as far as I know. The mother has long gone to be with the Lord.

Identification has removed the "old man" but that does not mean that you will not have problems. The ordinary problems of life still have to be faced. You will also have to face a hostile race. You will also have to face temptation. You will have to continue in the faith (Romans 11:22).

Now let us go back to Galatians 5. Before identification you were in verse 17. Now you are in verse 24. "And they that are Christ's have crucified the flesh with the affections and lusts."

To those who question whether or not this is a second definite work of grace, I will say No: Everything we receive from God is through grace. The first work of grace is usually salvation. I say usually because I have seen people healed before they were saved. It was a definite work of grace. Then they received the baptism of the Holy Spirit.

This was a third work of grace. We do not number. Who can tell where one work of grace begins and another ends?

Now you have put off the "old man". Now you can deal with your<u>self.</u> Jesus made this startling declaration, "Whosoever will come after me, let him deny himself, and take up his cross, and follow me" (Mark 8:34). Do not forget you are still a person with a will and power of choice. You have been so long under the old master, sin, that some things have been deep-set in your life. You have developed ideas, habits and attitudes that must be dealt with. What we are talking about is simply plain selfishness. You will relearn how to face situations in which you will want to satisfy yourself instead of doing God's will in the matter.

We must come to the point of complete dependence on the Spirit of God. Jesus said, "I can of my <u>own</u> <u>self</u> do nothing…" (John 5:30). It is learning to do everything in His ability. In your housework, on the job, in the ministry, it is the Lord and I doing this. He is the Master of all. We are co-laborers with God. (1 Corinthians 3:9) You have put off the "old man," but you cannot put off self. Self is you. What you are doing is getting rid of selfishness.

It is giving up your own way for His way.

You may have formed a habit of dilly-dallying around on the job. The Spirit of God tells you that it is wrong. Whom do you listen to? Of course, the

Holy Spirit. Now you give your employer your best. If you are an employer and you would like to do something that would make more money for you but would infringe upon the rights of your employees, the Holy Spirit will check you. What are you going to do? Be fair with your employees. Both employees should treat each other as they would like to be treated in Christ.

As a newborn babe, God does not reveal all things in your life that need to be corrected. But as He reveals each thing to you, correct it. He performs metamorphosis in you, and you take another step into a greater glory. It might be beneficial to read 2 Corinthians 3:18 again. Going from glory to glory does not particularly mean going from something to be corrected to better. It will be also going from a glorious state to a more glorious state. You see, making corrections in your life need not be an endless process. It is God's desire that you live a blameless and harmless, holy life. See Ephesians 1:4 and Philippians 2:15.

Identification has not ended with the putting off of the "old man". You must understand that you have put on a new man, as we have pointed out above in your union with Christ, which is the new creation. What is the "new man" like? We have enumerated the works of the "old man" on page 17.

Now we will present the <u>Fruit</u> of the <u>Spirit</u> which characterizes the new man.

Galatians 5:22-23	
Love	Goodness
Joy	Faith
Peace	Meekness
Longsuffering	Temperance
Gentleness	

There is a special lesson on the "Fruit of the Spirit" which will be studied in depth at another time.

What are the <u>works</u> of the new man?

"For we are his workmanship, created in Christ Jesus unto good works, which God hath before ordained that we should walk in them" (Eph. 2:10).

"Let your light shine before men, that they may see your good works and glorify your Father which is in heaven (Matthew 5:16).

"As we have therefore opportunity, let us do good unto all men, especially unto them who are of the household of faith (Gal. 6:10).

Love your enemies (Matthew 5:44-48).

Bless them that curse you.

Do good to them that hate you.

Pray for them that despitefully use you and persecute you.

Recompense to no man evil for evil.

Provide things honest in the sight of all men (Romans 12:9, 17).

    The believer is to bear fruit. Of what does this fruit consist? What is its relationship to works? "Now he that ministereth seed to the sower both minister bread for your food, and multiply your seed sown, and increase the fruits of your righteousness" (2 Corinthians 9:10). The context of this scripture is giving. "Every man according as he purposeth, so let him give; not grudgingly, or of necessity: for God loveth a cheerful giver" (2 Corinthians 9:7). Giving cheerfully is a fruit.

    Can "fruits" and "good works" be used interchangeably? The Philippians sent Paul a gift to help him in his ministry. His response was, "Not because I desire a gift: but I desire fruit that may abound to your account" (Philippians 4:17). Here a "good work" is called a "fruit". "That ye walk worthy of the Lord unto all pleasing, being <u>fruitful</u> in every <u>good</u> <u>work</u>, and increasing in the knowledge of

God' (Colossians 1:10). "Now there was at Joppa a certain disciple called Tabitha, which by interpretation is called Dorcas: this woman was full of good works, and almsdeeds which she did" (Acts 9:36). "Being filled with the fruits of righteousness, which are by Jesus Christ, unto the glory and praise of God" (Philippians 1:11). Jesus is "made unto us wisdom" (1 Corinthians 1:30). "But the wisdom that is from above is first pure, then peaceable, gentle, and easy to be entreated, full of mercy and good fruits, without partiality, and without hypocrisy" (James 3:17). It is obvious that the terms "fruit" and "good works" are interchangeable. We are to be "prepared unto every good work" (2 Timothy 2:21). We are to "bring forth fruit" (Colossians 1:6).

Good works are the outworking of Love. It is love in action. It is the fruit of the Spirit manifesting itself in action. It carries a reward. "For the Son of man shall come in the glory of his Father with his angels; and then he shall reward every man according to his works" (Matthew 16:27). It is laying up treasure in heaven. "But lay up for yourselves treasures in heaven…" (Matthew 6:19).

Identification with Jesus includes identifying with Him in good works. Jesus went about doing good" (Acts 10:38).

Another good work is the careful dispensing of what others give to you and its use. This is especially true if you are in a position of ministry. "When therefore I have performed this, and have sealed to them this fruit, I will come by you into Spain" (Romans 15:28). The people had given Paul a donation for the poor saints at Jerusalem. "When therefore I have sealed to them this fruit" arouses a question. Does it mean that a fruit (giving) to be sealed to the giver must be used properly? Would the fruit have been sealed if Paul had wasted some of it or improperly used it? We had better be sure that what we give is used properly if we expect to have it sealed to us. If you're going to give to a cause, it would be good to know how much of what you give really goes to those for whom it is intended or for the use it is intended.

Another question you may ask is, "What about my mind? What happened to it?" The first thing to consider is Romans 8:7, "Because the carnal (unregenerate) mind is enmity against God: for it is not subject to the law of God, neither indeed can be." This is the state of mind of the person who is in the "flesh," that is, his nature is under the power of sin. The change in your mind is given in Romans 12:2, "And be not conformed to this world: but be ye transformed by the renewing of your mind."

The word "transformed" is the Greek word "metamorphosis". An example of a metamorphosis is the changing of a caterpillar into a butterfly. Your mind is changed from carnal to spiritual by a metamorphosis performed by the Holy Spirit. You now have the mind of Christ. "But we have the mind of Christ" (1 Corinthians 2:16). "But ye are not in the flesh (your nature under the power of sin) but in the Spirit, if so be that the Spirit of God dwell in you" (Romans 8:9). Continue in the faith by living and walking in the Spirit (Romans 11:22 and Galatians 5:25).

"Please explain how I can continue in the Faith and live and walk in the Spirit." "…The inward man is renewed day by day" (2 Corinthians 4:16). How does this happen? Let us illustrate. How is your physical body renewed each day? It is done by eating food each day. This renews worn-out cells and renews your strength. It is the same for your inner man. There is one difference, however. Your outer man, the physical body, eventually runs down and dies. It is not so with your inner man. What is the food for the inner man? It is the Word of God. Read and study your Bible diligently each day. It is your food for the inner man.

Another thing that contributes to a healthy, growing, spiritual life is daily prayer. "Pray without ceasing" (1 Thessalonians 5:17). This does not mean that you have to be on your knees all the time. It is the attitude of the heart. It is living in constant consciousness of God dwelling within. "I will dwell in them and walk in them; and I will be their God, and they shall be my people" (2 Corinthians 6:16). "By him therefore let us offer the sacrifice of praise to God continually, that is, the fruit of your lips giving thanks to his name" (Hebrews 13:15). "How can I do that when my work demands a lot of concentration?" "Commit thy works unto the Lord, and thy thoughts shall be established" (Proverbs 16:3). "And whatever ye do, do it heartily, as to the Lord, and not unto men" (Colossians 3:23). As an example, Paul made tents while preaching (Acts

18:3). Working did not detract from Paul's spiritual life or power. While working to support himself he testifies, "Truly the signs of an apostle were wrought among you in all patience, in signs, and wonders, and mighty deeds" (2 Corinthians 12:12). A person holding the office of a deacon, a table waiter, can be a man of power. "And Stephen, full of faith, and power, did great wonders among the people" (Acts 6:8). He had been appointed a deacon in the early church. Your working will be no hindrance to God operating through you if you commit it all to Him.

    A third thing that contributes to a healthy spiritual life is confession. I do not mean confession of sins. I mean a good confession of Christ before mankind. I refer to your testimony of God's grace to those about you. The epistles tell of another, deeper type of prayer and worship which contributes to the building up of our spiritual lives. It is the practice of praying, speaking, and worshipping in the Holy Spirit. Jude says in verse 20, "But ye beloved, building up yourselves on your most holy faith, praying in the Holy Ghost." Ephesians 6:18 says, "Praying always with all prayer and supplication in the Spirit". See also 1 Corinthians 14:14.
You are a growing believer. God is delighted in you. He is signing over you with joy.

You are becoming like His Son, Jesus.

Identification with Christ involves many things:

Identification with Christ in **spirit.**

This we have seen in the union of your purified human nature and his divine nature. "He that is joined to the Lord is one spirit" (1 Corinthians 6:17).

Identification with Christ in **love.**

This with the above identification in spirit form the basis for all other.

You are commanded to love and to be compassionate:

Toward God: "Thou shalt love the Lord thy God… (Matthew 22:37).

Toward People: "Thou shalt love thy neighbor as thyself" (Matthew 22:39). This includes your enemies, sinners, friends, and all Christians.

Jesus' compassion always resulted in action that is in deliverance. (Mark 1:41, Matthew 14:14)
How can I do that?

God teaches you. "…Ye yourselves are taught of God to love one another" (1 Thessalonians 4:9).

"...The love of God is shed abroad in our hearts by the Holy Ghost which is given unto us" (Romans 5:5).

It is not mere human love, but you are loving with God's love. He gives you power to do His will.

It is to be a perfect love. "God is love; and he that dwelleth in love dwelleth in God, and God in him. Herein is our love made perfect....Perfect love casteth out fear..." (1 John 4:16-19). See also Matthew 5:43-48.

Identification with Christ in **body**.

Now ye are the body of Christ, and members in particular" (1 Corinthians 12:27).

"For we are members of his body, of his flesh, and of his bones" (Ephesians 5:30).

"For ye are bought with a price: therefore, glorify God in your body, and in your spirit, which are God's (1 Corinthians 6:20).

Jesus ministered in a physical body. He was the visible image of the invisible God (Hebrews 1:3). He needs another body through which to minister to the last. That body is you and me, individually and collectively. You are now the visible image of the invisible Christ.

Jesus said, "I am the vine, ye are the branches…" (John 15:5). The branches cannot bear fruit without the vine, He needs you, and you need him. This illustration shows the interdependence between Christ and His body, the church.

Identification with Christ in **His sufferings**.

If "we suffer with him…" (Romans 8:17).

"But rejoice, inasmuch as ye are partakers of Christ's sufferings" (1 Peter 4:13). See also 2 Thessalonians 1:5 and Philippians 1:29.

What must I suffer?

Tribulation. "In the world ye shall have tribulation" (John 6:33). The word, "tribulation," in the Greek means "pressure," such as the pressures brought against you by evil people. It includes, "Yes, and all that will live godly in Christ Jesus shall suffer persecution" (2 Tim. 3:12). Jesus never suffered from sickness or disease or any abnormal physical, emotional, mental, or other conditions. On the cross, He bore our sins and sicknesses. So, they are not a part of suffering with Him.

In 2 Corinthians 11:23-28, you will find a partial list of Paul's sufferings. The kind and amount of suffering you have to go through depends upon what kind of society you live in. All God asks is that you be faithful in what does come your way.

Identifying with Christ in **self-denial.**

"If any man will come after me, let him deny himself…" (Matthew 16:24). Jesus was not selfish. He wants us to get rid of all selfishness. Cease living for yourself and live only for Him. Jesus made this plain when He said, "I seek not my own will, but the will of the Father that sent me" (John 5:30). You are not to seek your own will anymore but the will of God.

"For even Christ pleased not himself" (Romans 15:3). Even so you please your "neighbor for his good to edification" (building up) (Romans 15:2).

"I can of my own self do nothing…" (John 5:30). In self-denial we repeat the same: "I can do nothing of myself." In everything it is doing His will.

"I must work the works of him that sent me" (John 9:4). We identify with this in our self-denial by saying, "I must do the will of the Lord in all things."

There is a surprise in this. You will find such a peace and joy and satisfaction in doing His will that living for self will fade into insignificance.

Identifying with Christ in the **cross.**

If any man will come after me, let him deny himself, and take up his cross and follow me" (Matthew 16:24).

What is my cross? It is closely linked with self-denial.

Jesus did not suffer on His cross for Himself but for us.

Our cross then is not for ourselves but for others.

It is the suffering of compassion for others.
It is pouring out strength to help others.
It is weeping with them that weep (Romans 12:15).
"Bear ye one another's burdens" (Galatians 6:2).
"Greater love hath no man than this, that a man <u>lay down</u> his life for his friends (John 15:13). It is giving up your own way or your own thing to help another.

It also carries over to enemies.

"Bless them that curse you,"
"Do good to them that hate you,"
"Pray for them that despitefully use you". (Matt. 5:44)
Leave vengeance to the Lord. See Romans 12:19

"And follow me" (Matthew 16:24). In all the above you will be following Jesus.

Identifying with Him and **His faith.**

"But without faith it is impossible to please him: for he that cometh to God must believe that He is, and that he is a rewarder of them that diligently seek him" (Hebrews 11:6).

Believe that God is, and you have taken Him at His word and entered into His family.

"…Your faith growth exceedingly…" (2 Thessalonians 1:3). There is growth in faith. How does it grow? The more you learn of the promises of God, the more your faith will grow. You will see how much God wants you to have. In faith you will reach out and take those promises. It is like a father telling his little son what he is going to get for him. Some of the things may be staggering to the little fellow. He may even remark, "Really, dad?" The father assures him, and the son believes it. How do you think the father would feel if the little boy would go to his mother and ask her to help him believe that his dad would do as he had said, especially if the father was a man of his word? "Help me, mom, to believe my dad." Yet, that is how people treat their heavenly Father who has never broken His word. Let us believe Him and stand firm.

What is the measure of faith that I may obtain or grow into? "…Nothing shall be impossible unto you" (Matthew 17:20). "Have faith in God" (the margin reads, "Have the faith of God") (Mark 11:22). God is a faith God. That is the ultimate in the growth of your faith. It is attainable. If it were not, these scriptures would not be in the Book. God does not speak idle words.

Identify with Jesus in **His rest.**

"There remaineth therefore a rest to the people of God. For he that is entered into his rest, he also hath ceased from his own works, as God did from his. Let us labor therefore to enter into that rest…" (Hebrews 4:9-11). The word, "labor", in the Greek means "to use speed."

How can I tell when I have entered into that rest? When you have ceased from your own works. "Forasmuch then as Christ hath suffered in the flesh, arm yourselves likewise with the same mind: for he that hath suffered in the flesh hath ceased from sin; that he no longer should live the rest of his time in the flesh (physical body) to the lust of men, but to the will of God" (1 Peter 4:1, 2). To cease from ones' own works means to cease from sin. Before you were saved, all your righteousness was as filthy rags in God's sight (Isaiah 64:6). There is a suffering involved in denying self. In all the process of identification you arrive at the place where you lay aside your will, your disposition, your desires, your temper, your likes and dislikes, and accept as yours Christ's will, Christ's disposition, Christ's temper, Christ's desires, Christ's likes and dislikes; then you have ceased from your own works. You have entered into the full rest of God.

What about this suffering?

I cannot tell you what it is in any detail. I do not know how willing you will be to go all the way with the Lord. I do not know how God will test you to see if you mean it when you make a total consecration. I do not know what tests will come your way to show up your needs so that the Spirit can change (metamorphose) your inner man. I will assure you that the more willing you are the less will be the suffering.

You are being given a lot to digest and assimilate. In writing history, one section will deal with the agriculture of a people, another with the culture, and another with architecture, etc. Yet, even though they are dealt with in different sections, they take place at the same time. It is true also of what is being written here. There are great overlaps and things that take place at the same time. You are growing in faith, in love, and in knowledge. These all are going on at the same time. These identifications do not follow in any particular order. Being changed from glory to glory carries all the way through.

Further identifications:

Identifying with Jesus in **His purity or holiness.**

"And every man that hath this hope (Jesus' coming) in him purifieth himself, even as he (Jesus) is pure" (1 John 3:3). That you can be pure is shown by the verse, "Seeing ye have purified your souls in obeying the truth through the Spirit…" (1 Peter 1:22). Peter writes, "I will stir up your pure minds" (2 Peter 3:1).

Now the end of the commandment is charity out of a pure heart…" (1 Timothy 1:5). Note: Charity out of a pure heart. There is no hindrance to the flow of God's love from a heart that is pure.

"…But follow righteousness, faith, charity, peace with them that call on the Lord out of a pure heart" (2 Timothy 2:22). "…Truly our fellowship is with the Father, and with His Son Jesus Christ" (1 John 1:3). It is easy and lovely to have fellowship with those who are pure in heart. They don't have something they are hanging onto for which they have to make excuse.

"Blessed are the pure in heart: for they shall see God" (Matt. 5:8). As the Holy Spirit guides you into all truth He will reveal the faults or things that need to be corrected in your life. You are not put under condemnation for that which has not been revealed to you directly by the Spirit or through one of the ministries as mentioned in Ephesians 4:11-13. You are pure and being made pure. You are perfect and being made perfect.

Identification with Him **"as He is."**

"Herein is our love made perfect that we may have boldness in the day of judgment: because as he is, so are we in this world" (1 John 4:17). He is the resurrected, triumphant, exultant Son of God.

"And hath raised us up together and made us sit together in heavenly places in Christ Jesus" (Ephesians 2:6). Where is He seated? "…And set him at his own right hand in the heavenly places, far above all principality, and power and might, and position in Christ." We share in His victory. He is our victory. When you accepted Him into your life, He brought His victory with Him. Now you operate from the standpoint of victory and not to victory. You have His ability and power to rule in every circumstance. You are not the victim but the victor. "…We are more than conquerors" (Romans 8:37). Why more? We have the victory before the battle starts. Satan knows this, but he hopes that you don't. When you realize that you are seated with Him far above all principality, power, might and dominion, then you will realize that fear of the devil is nonsense. You are above him.

Identification with **His authority and power.**

"All power is given unto me in heaven and in earth" (Matt. 28:18). Jesus, the head of His body (the church), has all power. The body shares in the power of the head.

"Behold, I give unto you power to tread on serpents and scorpions, and over all the power of the enemy: and nothing shall by any means hurt you" (Luke 10:19).

You have power over the devil.

Resist him and he has to flee. (James 4:7)
You do not have to give place to him. (Ephesians 4:27)
You have an invincible armor with a shield of faith that quenches all the fiery darts (missiles) of the wicked, the devil. (Ephesians 6:14-18)

"…Whatsoever ye shall ask of the Father in my name, He will give it you" (John 16:23). He gives us the use of His Name.

There is power in His Name. We act in the authority of His Name. You will cast out devils in His Name (Mark 16:17). You will lay hands on the sick in His Name and they shall recover. (Mark 16:18) "In His Name" means acting in Him. You are in Him and He is in you. (John 15:4) Jesus said, "…Without me ye can do nothing?" (John 15:5). You can do nothing outside of Jesus that will please God. Abide in Him, and you can say, "I can do all things through Christ which strengtheneth me" (Philippians 4:13).

In Him you have power to "reign in life" now. (Romans 5:17)

You have power to reign and rule your emotions.

You have power to rule your own spirit. (Proverbs 16:32)

You have power to control your God-given drives, such as hunger, sex, thirst, etc. You have power to avoid desiring to fulfill them out of God's order. One of the meanings of the word "power" (exousia) is superhuman. You are superhuman because you can reign successful in your life with Him. "Nothing shall by any means hurt you" (Luke 10:19). This is protection from the diseases, sicknesses, contaminated water and food, and demon power. You have power to witness.

Identification with Jesus in **His Ministry.**

"But ye shall receive power, after that the Holy Ghost is come upon you: and ye shall be witnesses…" (Acts 1:8)

"All power" in heaven and earth is given to Jesus. (Matt. 28:18) Now that you have received the Holy Spirit, you have the power to fulfill the Great Commission, 'Go…and teach" (Matt. 28:19-20).

"For he whom God hath sent speaketh the words of God: for God giveth not the Spirit by measure unto him" (John 3:34). Our Father does not expect you to go out to fulfill the commission with less equipment than Jesus had. You share in the authority and power of the head. Therefore, expect to receive the Spirit without measure. The flow of the Spirit will be great enough to meet every need and occasion.

"He that believeth on me, the works that I do shall he do also; and greater works than these shall he do…" (John 14:12). We need more of this kind of believer today. Set your sights on the ultimate in God. This does not always mean that you will be a great evangelist. It does mean that in your setting or community you should be able to meet the needs of those about you.

God said, "I will dwell in them, and walk in them" (2 Cor. 6:16).

God dwells in you.
He is looking out through your eyes and desiring to get the Word to that neighbor, to this person or that person.

God is in you.

He desires to lay hands on that sick person. Your hands are His hands. He bought your body with a great price (1 Corinthians 6:20). Get with it.

"I shall come in the fullness of the blessing of the gospel of Christ" (Romans 15:29). Present a full-rounded gospel. Leave nothing out. Do not compromise, not even for the sake of unity. Preach the whole truth and nothing but the truth. Be determined not to know anything among you, save Jesus Christ, and him crucified" (1 Corinthians 2:2).

Move, speak, and testify as God directs you. Let Him be your leader and commander. "Thou therefore endure hardness as a good soldier of Jesus Christ" (2 Timothy 2:3).

Identifying with Him in **His Purpose.**

"God…now commandeth all men everywhere to repent" (Acts 17:30).

Now you are identifying with His great purpose. He desires to take a people out for His Name, both Jew and Gentile. He will save all who will let Him. He is "not willing that any should perish, but that all should come to repentance" (2 Peter 3:9). "Him that cometh to me I will in no wise cast out" (John 6:37).

"For we are laborers together with God…" (1 Corinthians 3:9). We are part and parcel of His great purpose.

"…The true worshippers shall worship the Father in spirit and in truth: for the Father seeketh such to worship him" (John 4:23,24). We are laborers together with God in seeking worshippers. It is to bring glory to God. "…That God in all things may be glorified through Jesus Christ, to whom be praise, and dominion forever and ever" (1 Peter 4:11).

Identification with Christ in **His Travail.**

He shall see the travail of his soul, and shall be satisfied…" (Isaiah 53:11). The believer and the Lord are one spirit (1 Corinthians 6:17). In prayer the believer often travails with tears and in agony for the lost and for other believers whom may be in any trouble. "Weep with them that weep" (Romans 12:15).

The wife of my former pastor admonished us never to give up when praying for people. She and her husband had been praying for years for the salvation of a friend. Many years passed and now he was old and sick unto death. But he could not die, though the doctors said he should have been dead a year. Their prayers held death away from the man. One day he came to the end of himself and fell down before God in the hospital bathroom and repented. Jesus came into is heart, raised him up, and let him live for a time as a testimony of God's goodness. They travailed in prayer for this man and were satisfied.

The purpose of travailing in prayer is not to get God's attention to have Him do something. He is always ready to save. Travailing in prayer is one of the weapons of warfare against the devil. (2 Corinthians 10:4). It pulls the blinders off the eyes of the lost, so they can see Jesus and accept Him.

Identification with Jesus in **His intercession.**

"…Seeing he ever liveth to make intercession for them" (Heb. 7:25) We share in His intercessory ministry. "I exhort therefore, that, first of all, supplications, prayers, intercessions, and giving of thanks, be made for all men" (1 Timothy 2:1)

Many times, we are burdened in our hearts to pray for someone's deliverance. We may, or we may not, know for whom we are praying. It is a vital matter to pray earnestly until the burden lifts because someone's life may depend on that prayer of intercession. A mother was awakened in the night with a burden to pray for her son. She had no idea what was wrong. At the time she was praying, her son, who was on a merchant marine ship, was struck by lightning and was laid aside for dead. He came back to life because of intercessory prayer. We know of numerous cases in which peoples' lives have been spared by someone's intercessory prayer. The subject of intercessory prayer will be studied in detail in the special lesson.

Identification with Jesus in **character.**

"…As he is, so are we in this world" (1 John 4:17). It is to be Christ-like in our disposition, wants, desires, likes and dislikes, attitudes, etc. The character of Christ is manifested in, and can be seen through, the "fruit of the Spirit". Galatians 5:22, 23. This will be studied in a separate lesson because it is such a large subject.

You will identify with Jesus in **His return to rule on earth.**

"For the Lord himself shall descend from heaven with a shout, and with the voice of the archangel, and with the trump of God: and the dead in Christ shall rise first: then we which are alive and remain shall be caught up together with them in the clouds, to meet the Lord in the air…" (1 Thessalonians 4:15-18).

"…And the Lord my God shall come, and all the saints with thee" (Zechariah 14:5).

"And the armies which were in heaven followed him upon white horses…" (Revelation 19:11-14). Caught up to meet him; return with Him riding on white horses; what a great time lies ahead.

SANCTIFICATION

"But of him are ye in Christ Jesus, who of God is made unto us wisdom, and righteousness, and sanctification, and redemption" (1 Corinthians 1:30).
Sanctification is a very important part of the work of God in us. Jesus prayed that we would be sanctified. "Sanctify them through thy truth: thy word is truth" (John 17:17).
Let us define the terms:
Sanctify means to separate and cleanse. Sanctification means "purification, i.e. (the state) purity. The word "sanctification" and the word

"holiness" found in Hebrews 12:14, is the same word in the Greek text. "Follow peace with all men, and holiness, without which no man shall see the Lord." We have taken you through a study on identification. It is another term that has been substituted for sanctification in our study of putting off the "old man" and in living a pure life. To the degree you are like Jesus, to that degree you are a possessor of sanctification or holiness. Sanctification is the will of God. (1 Thessalonians 4:3)

We are sanctified by God the Father. (Jude 1)
It is through the truth. (John 17:19).
Jesus is the truth. (John 14:6).
It is of the Spirit. (2 Thessalonians 2:13 and 1 Peter 1:2)

Means of Sanctification.

It is through faith (Acts 26:18).
It is through the offering of the body of Jesus (Hebrews 10:10).
It is with the blood of Jesus (Hebrews 13:12).

Texts that prove you can be wholly sanctified (be like Jesus).

"And the very God of peace sanctify you wholly; and I pray God your whole spirit and soul and body be preserved blameless unto the coming of the Lord" (1 Thessalonians 5:23).

It is being sanctified, not at the coming or after the coming, but <u>unto</u> the coming of the Lord.

Acts 26:18, "…Are sanctified in me". "Are sanctified" shows that an act took place in the past and the action is still good.

1 Thessalonians 4:4, "That every one of you should know how to possess his vessel in sanctification and honor." If you could not enter into a state of sanctification (purity), how could you possess your vessel in sanctification?

1 Corinthians 1:2, "…To them that are sanctified…" Not everyone in the Corinthian church was sanctified; some were still in the process.

Hebrews 10:29, "…And counted the blood of the covenant wherewith he was sanctified…" "Was sanctified" is the past tense.
      Sanctification and holiness are having a pure heart. The very term "sanctification" brings an objection from some. It has been a controversial subject. Some have wrongly taught that a totally sanctified person could not sin. He still as a free will and power of choice. "Lie not one to another, seeing that ye had put off the old man with his deeds" (Colossians 3:9). Adam didn't have the "old man," but he chose to sin. Some say a totally sanctified man could not be tempted. He can. Jesus was tempted, and I am sure no one will deny that He was a sanctified man.

I know that I am going to spend eternity with the Lord. What is the subject of this study for me as I live in this world? What does it mean for me now?"

Some objectives:

Your testimony backed by a godly life to the glory of God.

That ye may be blameless and harmless, the sons of God, without <u>rebuke</u>, in the midst of a crooked and perverse nation, among whom ye shine as lights in the world" (Philippians 2:15). "Ye are the light of the world" (Matthew 5:14).

That ye may walk worthy of the vocation. (Ephesians 4:1)

That His will be done on earth as it is in heaven (in your life). (Matt. 6:10)
That you may be effective witnesses for Him (Acts 1:8).

That we may in fact be the salt of the earth (Matthew 5:13).

That we may not be ashamed before Him at His coming (1 John 2:28).
That we may be ready when Jesus comes (Matthew 24:44).

That the world may see Jesus in us (Colossians 1:27). You may be the only Bible some will ever read.

That we may bring glory to God (1 Corinthians 10:31).

That you might grow up into Him in all things (Ephesians 4:15).
    The great objective of all of the epistles in particular is to bring us into living a pure life and to continue living a pure life. There is no such thing as attaining and then stopping. We must continue to run the race with patience (Hebrews 12:1, 2).

Continue:

"But continue thou in the things which thou hast learned and has been assured of…" (2 Timothy 3:14).

"Take heed unto thyself, and unto the doctrine; continue in them…" (1 Timothy 4:16).

"If ye continue in my word, then are ye my disciples indeed" (John 8:31).

"…Continue ye in my love" (John 15:9).

"If ye continue in the faith grounded and settled…" (Colossians 1:23).

"...But toward thee goodness, if thou continue in his goodness: otherwise thou also shalt be cut off" (Romans 11:22). The fruitless branch is cut out of the vine. (John 15:4-7)

The warning:

"Therefore, we ought to give the more earnest heed to the things which we have heard, lest at any time we should let them slip" (Heb. 2:1-3).

"What in particular is the danger? Who would know if I slipped?"
"Be sober, be vigilant; because your adversary the devil, as a roaring lion walketh about seeking whom he may devour: whom resist steadfast in the faith..." (1 Peter 5:8, 9).

If you let the Word and the operation of it in your lives slip, you are not being sober nor vigilant. Satan will take advantage of the laying down of your shield of faith and will do everything he can to tear up and destroy your life. Don't say what comes as a result is of God or was allowed of God. It was your own choice to slip, so what comes is a result of that choice. When you have had enough of the devil, God stands ready to forgive and to help you.

"I must continue to live a pure and godly life. Can you give me a few verses to help me?"

Jesus said these very wonderful words: "Behold, I give unto you power to tread on serpents and scorpions, and over all the power of the enemy…" (Luke 10:19). On the basis of this statement, coupled with "…Greater is he that is in you, than he that is in the world" (1 John 4:4), you have all the resources of heaven behind you. Now you can say, "I can do all things through Christ which strengtheneth me" (Philippians 4:13).

There are some "keeps" that should be considered.

"…Neither be partaker of other men's sins: <u>keep</u> thyself pure" (1 Timothy 5:22). When men ask you to join in doing wrong, refuse. The manner of your refusal and the words you use will be given you at the time for the occasion.
Pure religion and undefiled before God and the Father is this, to visit the fatherless and widows in their affliction, and to <u>keep</u> himself unspotted from the world."

Three things constitute the world. (1 John 2:15, 16).
The lust of the flesh. Do not allow the normal desires to be filled out of God's order. The lust of the eyes. Do not allow what you see to arouse desires in you for that which is wrong.

The pride of life. Do not let the devil rob you of your humility by a spirit of arrogance or an excessively high opinion of yourself. Love not these things, as they are of the world."Little children, keep yourselves from idols" (1 John 5:21). Anything one put ahead of God is an idol. Any substitute for the Lord is an idol. The most likely danger of a modern idol is materialism. Money can easily become an idol.

"Keep yourselves in the love of God…" (Jude 21).
You can choose to love. You can choose to hate. Always choose to love and reject hate. Agape love is largely a choice of the will. Compassion is a part or ingredient of agape love.

"That good thing which was committed unto thee keep by the Holy Ghost which dwelleth in us" (2 Timothy 1:14).

"We know that whosoever is born of God sinneth not; but he that is begotten of God keepeth himself, and that wicked one toucheth him not" (1 John 5:18).

"Keepeth himself." How does one do this? By putting on all the armor of God and by quenching all the fiery darts (missiles) of the devil. (Ephesians 6:13-18). Combined with the armor, and active faith and the radiation of the Holy Spirit from the believer make him impregnable to any touch of the devil. "Nothing shall by any means hurt you" (Luke 10:19).

The believer keeps himself by being sober and vigilant. (1 Peter 5:8, 9). He allows no loophole through which the devil can touch him.

The believer who quenches all the fiery darts of the devil will sin not. He will then be one with those of John's day. He or she can say, "And whatsoever we ask, we receive of him, because we keep his commandments, and do those things that are pleasing in his sight" (1 John 3:22). This is the key to <u>keeping</u>; God dwells in you. "Thou therefore, my son, be strong in the grace that is in Christ Jesus" (2 Timothy 2:1).

In the light of God's love and favor (grace) you can be strong, knowing that the grace of God is greater and more abundant. (Romans 5:17, 20, 21)

"Finally, my brethren, be strong in the Lord, and in the power of his might"
(Ephesians 6:10).

Make sure of your stand:

"Wherefore the rather, brethren, give diligence to make your calling and election sure: for if ye do these things, ye shall never fall" (2 Peter 1:10). You make your calling and election sure by knowing the Word.

You make your calling and election sure by putting the Word into practice.

You make your calling and election sure by always choosing His will.
    Now you know where you stand. You are going from glory to glory. God is delighted in you. He is singing over you with joy. Now you know where you stand. You know! You do not **think** you stand, you know it. "Wherefore let him that thinketh he standeth take heed lest he fall" (1 Corinthians 10:12). This scripture is directed to babes in Christ who too often just think they stand and are not sure of it. Now you are sure: you know. Your "sufficiency is of God" (2 Corinthians 3:5). "And hereby we do **know** that we **know** him, if we keep his commandments" (1 John 2:3). It is a part of the fulfillment in your life of 1 John 2:20, "And ye know all things".

INCARNATION

    The unifying nature of God and man is the crowning achievement of Jesus Christ. The reason for the cross was thus revealed: God in man and man in God, once and indissoluble, one mind, one purpose, one effort, one power, and one glory.
    You are born again by the Holy Spirit. Jesus, the Son of God, came into your life. "He that abideth in the doctrine of Christ, he hath both the Father and the Son" (2 John 9). "And I will pray the Father, and he shall give you another Comforter, that he may abide with you forever; even the Spirit of truth; whom the world cannot receive, because it seeth him not; for he dwelleth with you, and shall be

in you" (John 14:16, 17). He came in on the day of Pentecost and has been coming into everyone who will receive Him since. So, you have God dwelling in you. "I will dwell in them" (2 Corinthians 6:16).

God was in Christ, an incarnation. "To wit, that God was in Christ, reconciling the world unto himself..." (2 Corinthians 5:19). God is in you, "and hath committed unto us the word of reconciliation" (2 Corinthians 5:19). God is in you, an incarnation. Jesus is in you by imparting His nature to you. You also have the Holy Spirit. God dwells in you: that is an incarnation.

A young man once said, "There is one lesson on identification that thrilled me through and through. I laid your manuscript down and went about my daily business, but my mind kept coming back to it. I am going to read it over with all those scriptures every day." I wanted him to tell me why. He said, "I am going to do it for this reason. It is not mine yet. It is not a part of me. I remember when I took up Latin. I studied it for two years before Latin became mine, so that I could translate English into Latin and Latin into English..." He said, "Now I know about this incarnation. I know about this indwelling of God. I know my legal rights, but it is not mine yet in a practical way so I can use it. The devil has me at a disadvantage still, but I will yet stand before the devil just as Jesus stood before the devil."[1]

This young man had the new birth. He was filled with the Holy Spirit. Now he was learning

---
[1] "Incarnation" by Rev. John G. Lake

about identification. It opened a whole new realm of reality to him. He needed to grasp the reality of it until it became a part of him. You may have eternal life. You are a new creation (2 Corinthians 5:17). You are now a son or daughter of God (1 John 3:2). You are a life child. You are both a child by birth and by adoption. You are a blood child with God's nature in you.

What do we know? Do we just believe it is so? Is it real that God truly dwells in me? In you there is a union of the uncreated God with you, a created man or woman. You know that. It is amazing to note that in the short five chapters of 1 John the expression, "we know" appears 26 times. It is passing from a stage of just believing it is so to a stage of <u>knowing</u> it is so.

You are born again. It is a fact. You know it.
The Bible is true. It is a fact. You know it.
You have eternal life. It is a fact. You know it.
The Holy Spirit is in you. It is a fact. You know it.
Christ is in you. It is a fact. You know it.
The Father dwells in you. It is a fact. You know it.
You are a member of His body. It is a fact. You know it.
You are a son. It is a fact. You know it.

You are in the family of God. You are a <u>believer</u>. You have a right to use the Name of Jesus.

It is just like having a pass. When I worked for the Great Northern Railroad one year, I had a pass. It entitled me to ride on the passenger train free. All I had to do was show that pass at the gate, and I was in. You see, I belonged to a definite system. You belong to a definite system. You are a member of Christ's body (Ephesians 5:30): "For we are members of his body, of his flesh, and of his bones."

You do not have to try to believe the Word. You are a believer. You do not have to try to be a son. You are a son of God.

"Greater is He that is in you, than he that is in the world" (1 John 4:4). …Christ in you, the hope of glory" (Colossians 1:27). Never think of yourself as being one place and Jesus another. He dwells in you, as incarnation. He is always in you. Think it, practice it, until you are conscious of His continuing presence.

Now you walk in the faith realm. Sight means reason. We walk by faith not by sight (2 Corinthians 5:7). You walk by faith, not by sight. Now you are a faith walker. Now you are in the class with Jesus. Jesus was a faith walker and worker. God is a faith God. When He wanted the earth, He spoke and it was. Through faith we understand that the worlds were framed by the Word of God, so that "things which are seen were not made of things which do appear" (Hebrews 11:3). All God had to do was speak the word and the world came into being. The faith in God is available to you. "Have faith in God." In the margin it says, "Have the faith of God" (Mark 11:22). Jesus said, "…Nothing shall be impossible unto you" (Matthew 17:20). Get the force of it. "...Walk, even as he walked" (1 John 2:6).

A woman came to Dr. Dowie with cancer in her mouth. Dr. Dowie put his finger on it and began to feel of it. Faith spoke to that cancer, and Dr. Dowie lifted it out of her mouth. What was that? Reason? Oh no, reason would say you must cut that out. Faith said it is dead. Dr. Dowie acted in Jesus' stead. He that was in Dr. Dowie was greater than the cancer.

Now you have the theory of this thing. Now in the Name of Jesus Christ you have seen the reality of it. Now go, and let this reality govern your life.

Let us summarize. You are in the family of God. You do not have to try to be that. You know you are in the family. You do not have to try to be a son of God. You know you are. You have all the authority of heaven and earth in the Name of Jesus. You do not have to try to exercise authority. "...Whatsoever thou shalt bind on earth shall be bound in heaven: and whatsoever thou shalt loose on earth shall be loosed in heaven" (Matthew 16:19). When you bind, heaven responds. When you loose, heaven responds. When you use the Name, heaven respects that Name and responds. You simply exercise authority in His wonderful, powerful Name.

He is in you. Let Him have His way.

The triumph of the gospel is enough to make any man the wildest kind of an enthusiastic optimist.

DOMINION
BIBLE INSTITUTE
TRAINING THE NEXT GENERATION OF GOD'S GENERALS
SIGN UP TODAY!
dbiaccounts@jglm.org
John G. Lake Ministries
SAME MESSAGE. SAME POWER. SAME RESULTS.

John G. Lake Ministries
Same Message. Same Power. Same Results.

Partner With Us As We Advance God's Kingdom On Earth!

Partner Benefits Include:
- Our monthly "Laboring Together" newsletter with a ministry update directly from Brother Curry that includes detailed information about our upcoming events and activities. We compile testimonies from all over the world to encourage and strengthen your faith.

- Partner E-Newsletter includes an MP3 every month taught by Brother Curry with the option to download our monthly audio teaching.

- 30% Discount on all products during the holiday season...

- Our Promise to Protect Your Kingdom Investment.

Partners can choose to receive packets by postal mail or via email. Your faithful support allows us to help give our materials away freely to those who cannot give, such as our JGLM prison ministries, disaster relief funds and foreign missionaries. Most importantly we depend on our faithful partners as our main line of prayer support.

Email: partners@jglm.org
www.jglm.org/partners

New Man
This Changes Everything...

The Primary focus of the DHT seminar is to train believers to biblically and effectively minister healing. The purpose of the New Man seminar is to reveal to believers what was accomplished by Jesus for us through His death, burial, and resurrection. The New Man Seminar reveals what you are (in Christ) not what you will some day become. It also reveals how to begin being who you are rather than emphasizing waiting for the next "Christian Fad".

John G. Lake Ministries
SAME MESSAGE. SAME POWER. SAME RESULTS.

Get Yours Today! Call **888-293-6591** or Visit Us Online: store.jglm.org

- You are left unsatisfied by the status quo...
- You know you were meant to be a participant and not just a spectator...
- You ask "Why not?..." more than "Why?"...
- You believe that today can be better than yesterday...
- You know you were meant to walk among the Giants of the Faith, and you want the tools & training that can make it happen...
- When you hear the exploits of God's Generals, you can picture yourself doing them...

If this describes you, then you ARE JGLM... whether you know it or not.

COME.
LET'S CHANGE THE WORLD.

John G. Lake Ministries
SAME MESSAGE. SAME POWER. SAME RESULTS.

LIFE TEAM
The Saints Army
lifeteams@jglm.org

Go out into all the world. Preach the gospel, heal the sick, cast out demons and make disciples

The Teaching That Birthed A Legend Is Now Raising An Army.

Get Yours Today
Call **888-293-6591**
or Visit Us Online

store.jglm.org

John G. Lake Ministries
SAME MESSAGE. SAME POWER. SAME RESULTS.